Keeping Time

Contents

Features

Find out how time is divided up in
Time Is . . . on page 5.

The word *calendar* has quite a lot to do with
numbers. Find out what the connection is
and where this word comes from on page 10.

Take a look at some clocks around the
world in **Famous Timepieces** on page 20.

Can you figure out what time it is in different
countries around the world? Use the clues on
page 25 to help.

How did the months get their names?

Visit www.rigbyinfoquest.com
for more about TIME.

What Is Time?

How many weeks until my birthday? Which day is Grandma coming? What time do I have to get up in the morning?

To answer such questions, you need to know about time. But what is time? We can watch the clock ticking off the minutes, but we can't see time itself. We can only see the changes that time brings. Time is something we share with everyone on Earth, so we need a common way of organizing and describing time.

A time line is used to record events over a period of time and to show how things change with time. By looking at a time line of Sam's art, we can see how his drawing has improved over four years.

Sam, age 4

Sam, age 6

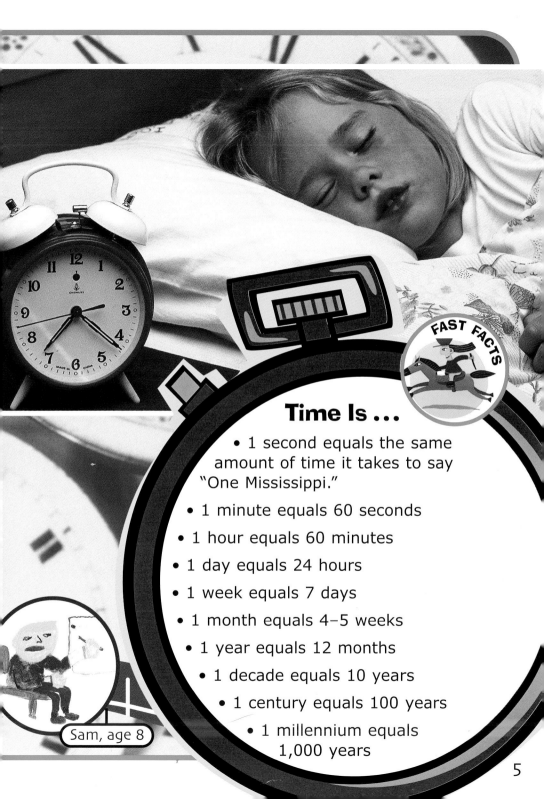

Time Is ...

- 1 second equals the same amount of time it takes to say "One Mississippi."

- 1 minute equals 60 seconds

- 1 hour equals 60 minutes

- 1 day equals 24 hours

- 1 week equals 7 days

- 1 month equals 4–5 weeks

- 1 year equals 12 months

- 1 decade equals 10 years

- 1 century equals 100 years

- 1 millennium equals 1,000 years

FAST FACTS

Sam, age 8

5

Nature's Time

Time has not always been measured in minutes, hours, weeks, and months. Long ago, people followed nature's time. They would eat when they were hungry and sleep when it got dark. They got up with the rising sun and worked while there was light.

The changing seasons gave a pattern to their lives. They watched the birds and other animals. They saw the trees change color, then drop leaves, and once more grow new leaves, blossoms, and fruit.

Nature has its own ways of measuring time. Some plants, such as water lilies, open and close at certain times of the day.

Each season brought new foods and a new time to early Native American people. In winter, they followed the journeys of caribou and other animals. In summer, they collected fruits, nuts, and berries.

Measuring Time

Finding a common way of measuring time became important as people began to settle in towns and villages. Early astronomers watched the cycle of the moon. They saw how the moon seemed to grow and shrink in the same cycle again and again. They observed the movement of the sun during the day, and the distance of the sun from Earth during the different seasons.

It is thought that the ancient Egyptians were the first to try figuring out how many days there were in a year. By watching the moon, they divided the year into 354 parts.

After skywatching for hundreds of years, people now know that it takes just over 365 days for Earth to travel around the sun. This makes one year.

Cycle of the moon

A group of large stones in England called Stonehenge is thought to be one of the oldest calendars in the world. Experts believe that ancient people used the stones to mark the positions of the sun and moon at the **summer solstice** and the **winter solstice.**

Counting the Days

Over the years, calendars have caused many arguments. Everyone had a different opinion of how many months and days there should be in a year. Many early calendars were based on the cycle of the moon. These calendars are called **lunar calendars.** The trouble with lunar calendars is that twelve lunar months adds up to only about 354 days. After many years, the calendars became mismatched with the seasons.

WORD BUILDER

Calendars keep count of the days just as account books are used to keep count of figures. It's not surprising then that the word *calendar* comes from the Latin for "account book"—*Kalendarium.*

This interesting carving is also a calendar. The ancient Aztecs of Central America carved this calendar in jade.

Believe It or Not!

This large stone pyramid built 1,000 years ago is actually a calendar! It was made by the ancient Mayans of Central America. The pyramid has four stairways, each with 91 steps, and a platform at the top, making a total of 365—the number of days in a calendar year.

SITESEEING
PAST & FUTURE

How did the months get their names?

Visit **www.rigbyinfoquest.com**
for more about TIME.

Changing Calendars

Nearly 1,950 years ago, a Roman emperor named Julius Caesar introduced the Julian calendar to the **Roman Empire**. The Julian calendar gave the year 365 days, split into twelve months. Unfortunately, Julius Caesar's calendar was off by eleven minutes and fourteen seconds.

In 1582, this problem was fixed. A new calendar called the Gregorian calendar was introduced by **Pope Gregory XIII**. After years of arguing, most Western countries adopted this calendar, although they all had to lose eleven days. This is the calendar we use today.

Julius Caesar

A Julian Calendar

When Julius Caesar introduced his calendar, the months of July and August were added to the year.

This is a French calendar from the 1400s. It shows the month of February.

11

THURSDAY

FRIDAY

3

IN FOCUS

Some calendars and clocks use Roman numerals. To read Roman numerals, just remember that the letter *I* equals 1, *V* equals 5, and *X* equals 10. If an *I* is before another letter, 1 is subtracted, so *IV* means 4. If an *I* comes after another letter, 1 is added, so *VI* means 6.

The Chinese Calendar

Many cultures have their own calendars and own special times. The Chinese New Year begins sometime between January 20 and February 20, whenever the second new moon of the northern winter appears. Each year takes its name from one of twelve animals. People born in that year are said to be similar in certain ways. After twelve years, the cycle begins again.

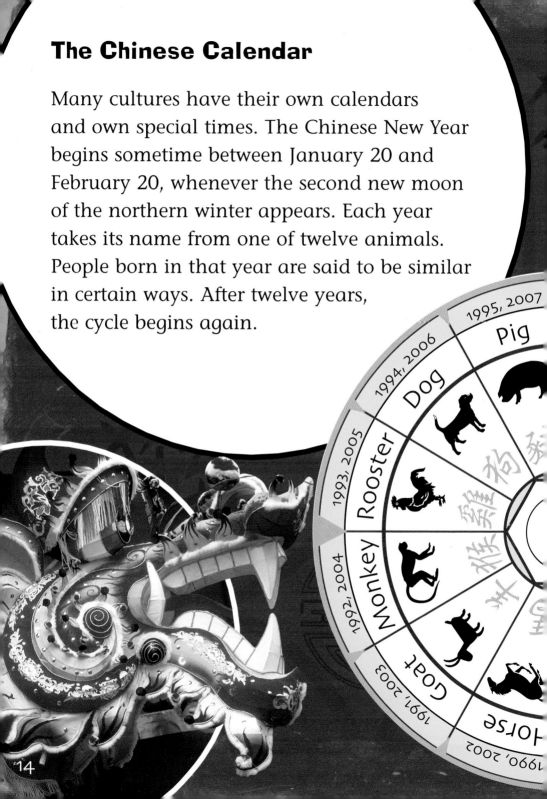

Find the year you were born on the circle below. This is your Chinese animal sign. Read the description of your sign on the right. Does this sound like you?

Rats are often very clever. Rats like to make the most of the situation they are in.

Oxen are honest, kind, hardworking, and reliable.

Tigers are leaders and take risks. They like excitement.

Rabbits are often caring. As children, they enjoy school and team sports.

Dragons are strong-willed. If they want to do something, they usually do it well.

Snakes are deep thinkers and give good advice. Home is a snake's favorite place.

Horses love to talk and spend time with their friends.

Goats are easy-going and always look for the best in people.

Monkeys have great imaginations and love contests.

Roosters are very friendly. They have many interests and hobbies.

Dogs like to help others. They make honest and loyal friends.

Pigs usually love reading, writing, and having fun.

1984, 1996
Rat

1985, 1997
Ox

1986, 1998
Tiger

1987, 1999
Rabbit

1988, 2000
Dragon

1989, 2001
Snake

15

Telling the Time

People had ways of telling the time long before **mechanical clocks** and watches were invented. The first clocks were probably sundials. Sundials use the sun's movement across the sky to tell the time. The sun casts a shadow that moves across the dial and points to the hours. The ancient Egyptians, Greeks, and Romans also used water, sand, candle, and rope clocks.

Some sundials are as small as a watch. Others are huge. This large sundial is in a public park in New Orleans, Louisiana.

Water Clock—A water clock was made with two pots, one with a hole in it. How much time had passed could be seen by how much water had drained from one pot to the other.

Sand Clock—A sand clock, or hourglass, had two glass bulbs joined by a small opening. One glass bulb was filled with sand. It took one hour for the sand to drain from one bulb to the other.

Candle Clock—A candle clock was simply a candle with marks on it. As the candle burned down to each mark, it measured that a set amount of time had passed.

Rope Clock—A rope clock was made from a rope with knots tied in it at regular spaces. The rope was soaked in water and lit. As the fire burned past each knot, a period of time was counted off.

Clocks and Watches

In Europe, the first mechanical clocks were in church bell towers. They had no face or hands but kept time by striking a bell every hour. Later, clock faces and hands were added so that people could see what the time was as well as hear the sound of the bell.

The first watches were made in Germany in the 1500s and were worn from belts or around the neck on a chain.

FAST FACTS

Women were the first to wear watches on their wrists. Men didn't wear watches on their wrists until the first World War when it became difficult for them to get to their pocket watches.

Digital clocks and watches show
the time in numbers, or digits.

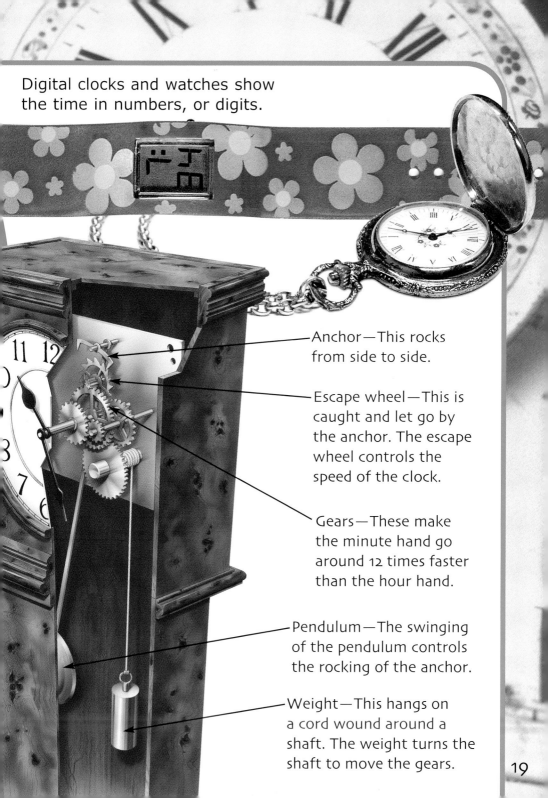

Anchor—This rocks
from side to side.

Escape wheel—This is
caught and let go by
the anchor. The escape
wheel controls the
speed of the clock.

Gears—These make
the minute hand go
around 12 times faster
than the hour hand.

Pendulum—The swinging
of the pendulum controls
the rocking of the anchor.

Weight—This hangs on
a cord wound around a
shaft. The weight turns the
shaft to move the gears.

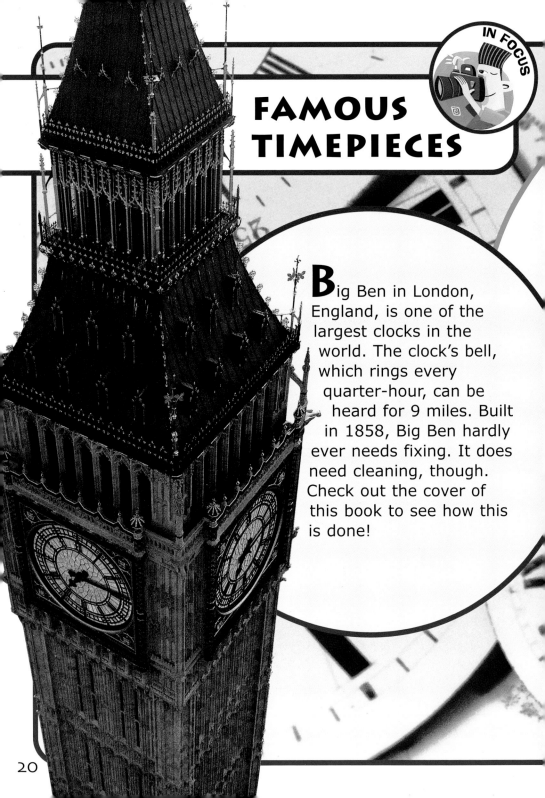

FAMOUS TIMEPIECES

Big Ben in London, England, is one of the largest clocks in the world. The clock's bell, which rings every quarter-hour, can be heard for 9 miles. Built in 1858, Big Ben hardly ever needs fixing. It does need cleaning, though. Check out the cover of this book to see how this is done!

One of the most interesting clocks in the world is the Astronomical Clock of Prague in the Czech Republic. This famous clock was built in 1410 and has been keeping time for six centuries. Every hour, twelve carved figures move and a rooster crows. As well as showing the hour, the clock also shows the positions of the sun, moon, and stars.

Legend says the rulers of Prague blinded the clockmaker so he couldn't make another clock as beautiful as theirs.

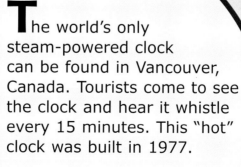

The world's only steam-powered clock can be found in Vancouver, Canada. Tourists come to see the clock and hear it whistle every 15 minutes. This "hot" clock was built in 1977.

What Time Is It?

For many centuries, people in every country of the world worked with their own local time, based on when the sun rose and set in their area. As travel increased in the 1800s, people became confused by different times in different places. Railroads needed standard timetables of departures and arrivals.

The British railway companies solved the problem by using the time at a place called Greenwich in all their stations. This time, which is called Greenwich mean time, was adopted by all of Great Britain.

Railway T

☞**LONDON T**
STOPPING AT A

STATION	A
WATERLOO	
BARNET	
ST. ALBANS	0
DUNSTABLE	0
NORTHAMPTON	1(
COVENTRY	12
LEICESTER	13
DERBY	14:
NOTTINGHAM	151
CHESTERFIELD	160
SHEFFIELD	164(
MANCHESTER	1800
BRADFORD	2010
LEEDS	2100

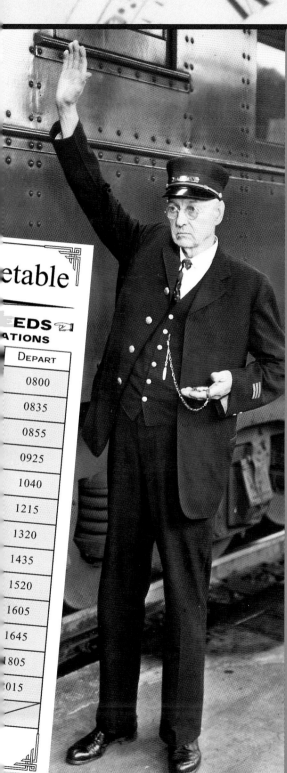

etable

EDS
ATIONS

DEPART
0800
0835
0855
0925
1040
1215
1320
1435
1520
1605
1645
1805
2015

Since 1852, people in Greenwich have told the time by the **twenty-four hour clock** outside the Greenwich Observatory. This clock always tells the right time as it is controlled by a special master clock. The master clock sends electrical signals once each second to make the Greenwich clock tick. People still set their watches to this special clock.

23

Your Time, My Time

In 1884, people from different countries held a meeting to make a standard time system around the world. They decided that Greenwich mean time would be the starting point for time everywhere else. The world was split into 24 time zones, each marked by a **meridian**.

The time is the same across each time zone, and it is one hour ahead of or behind the neighboring time zones. The international date line marks where one day ends and another begins.

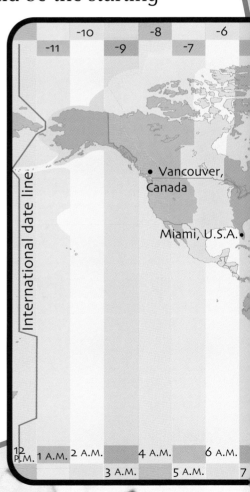

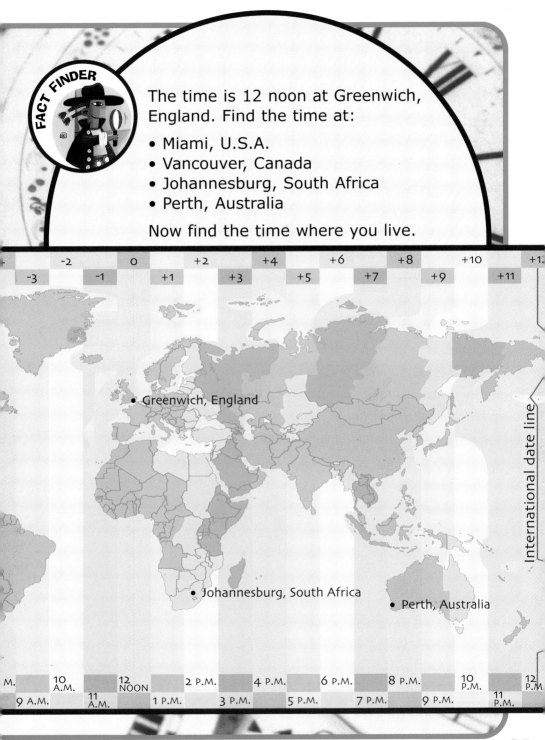

FACT FINDER

The time is 12 noon at Greenwich, England. Find the time at:

- Miami, U.S.A.
- Vancouver, Canada
- Johannesburg, South Africa
- Perth, Australia

Now find the time where you live.

-3   -2   -1   0   +1   +2   +3   +4   +5   +6   +7   +8   +9   +10   +11   +1.

Greenwich, England

Johannesburg, South Africa

Perth, Australia

International date line

M.   9 A.M.   10 A.M.   11 A.M.   12 NOON   1 P.M.   2 P.M.   3 P.M.   4 P.M.   5 P.M.   6 P.M.   7 P.M.   8 P.M.   9 P.M.   10 P.M.   11 P.M.   12 P.M

Timekeeping Today

Today, we have many different timekeepers. We wear watches and carry phones that display the time and the date. Our homes have digital clocks on microwaves, stoves, and televisions. We have ornamental clocks, grandfather clocks, and alarm clocks to wake us in the morning.

Calendars and diaries remind us of things we need to do and places we need to be. We have no excuse for being late, no time to spare, and no time on our hands!

The most accurate clocks in the world are atomic clocks (shown right). Invented in the United States in the 1950s, they gain or lose no more than a second in 1 million years. Because they are so accurate, atomic clocks are used in space travel.

Many skills and traditions can be lost or forgotten over time. To keep skills such as clockmaking alive, knowledge needs to be passed from older to younger people.

:00

FACT FINDER

Time Sayings

Can you find the meaning of the sayings below by following the grid references?

- Many moons ago. 8:00
- Work around the clock 8:45
- Till the cows come home . . 6:15
- In the nick of time 6:45
- Time flies 5:00
- Time will tell 3:45
- A stitch in time saves nine . 7:30
- Once in a blue moon 6:00
- Have time on your hands . . 4:45
- Time is a great healer 7:15

Time passes quickly

:15

:30

The truth will be shown sooner or later.

:45

Not having enough to do

:00

A long
time ago

Not very
often

Taking
a long time

:15

As time passes, things
will get better.

:30

Fix little problems now
to save time later.

Before
disaster
happens

To work many hours
without stopping

:45

Glossary

lunar calendar – a calendar based on twelve lunar months, or cycles of the moon. Each lunar month is about 29 ½ days long.

mechanical clock – a clock that is driven by a clockwork motor inside it rather than by electricity

meridian – an imaginary line that forms a circle around Earth from the top to the bottom

Pope Gregory XIII – the head of the Roman Catholic Church from 1572–1585

Roman Empire – the name used for the ancient Western world. The Roman Empire was ruled by powerful emperors who lived in Rome, Italy.

summer solstice – the longest day of the year. In the Northern Hemisphere, it is on June 20, 21, or 22. In the Southern Hemisphere, it is on December 21 or 22. This marks the beginning of summer.

twenty-four hour clock – a clock that is used to clearly show the difference between morning and evening hours. Using twenty-four hour time, 9:00 A.M. would be shown as 0900 and 9:00 P.M. would be shown as 2100.

winter solstice – the shortest day of the year. In the Northern Hemisphere, it is on December 21 or 22. In the Southern Hemisphere, it is on June 20, 21, or 22. This marks the beginning of winter.

Index

12-hour time	24-hour time
1 A.M.	0100
2 A.M.	0200
3 A.M.	0300
4 A.M.	0400
5 A.M.	0500
6 A.M.	0600
7 A.M.	0700
8 A.M.	0800
9 A.M.	0900
10 A.M.	1000
11 A.M.	1100
12 NOON	1200
1 P.M.	1300
2 P.M.	1400
3 P.M.	1500
4 P.M.	1600
5 P.M.	1700
6 P.M.	1800
7 P.M.	1900
8 P.M.	2000
9 P.M.	2100
10 P.M.	2200
11 P.M.	2300
12 P.M.	2400

Discussion Starters

1 Today, we have lots of different ways to measure the passing of time. However, the changing of the seasons is still very important. What are some of the things you do in summer, autumn, winter, and spring? Why do you do these things at these times of the year?

2 In 1752, most Western countries changed to the Gregorian calendar and lost eleven days. What would have been some of the problems caused by losing eleven days? What would be good about losing eleven days?

3 The first clocks were not very reliable. What do you think some of the timekeeping problems would have been with these clocks?
- sundials
- water clocks
- sand clocks
- rope clocks
- candle clocks